SCYTHING GRACE

SCYTHING GRACE

SEAN THOMAS DOUGHERTY

etruscan press

Etruscan Press
Wilkes University
84 West South Street
Wilkes-Barre, PA 18766
(570) 408-4546

WILKES UNIVERSITY

www.etruscanpress.org

Published 2013 by Etruscan Press
Printed in the United States of America
Cover Photograph by Cary Conover
Cover Design by Julianne Popovec
The text of this book is set in Adobe Garamond Pro.

First Edition

13 14 15 16 17 5 4 3 2 1

Please turn to the back of this book for a list of the sustaining funders of
Etruscan Press.

"Wherever I turn, wherever I look,
I see the black ruins of my life."

—C. P. Cavafy

"I dreamed a knife like a song you can't whistle."

—Frank Stanford

SCYTHING GRACE

Thanks to the editors of the following sites and journals, big and small, who first published these poems, sometimes in different versions:

2Bridges Review "Poem Not Titled Elegy in my Other Windowed Room"
Agni "Stenographer of the Damned"
Anti "Daily Architecture Without Hesitation"
A Narrow Fellow "Half Past 3 A.M."
Barely South "Canning Sardines (Slavic Grandma Holds the First Sky Over the Next)
Bitter Oleander "Orphaned"
The Bakery "Your Voice is a Right Cross"
Conduit "The Literacy of Longing," "An Arrival Like An Axle"
Copper Nickel "The Ongoing Elegy to Everything"
Cream City Review "Sonogram"
Filling Station (Canada) "Triptych from the Dictionary of Dead Letters"
Forklift (Ohio) "Poem Written in the Margin of an Eclipse," "Untranslatable Autobiography or Employment Application That Ends in Birds"
Fur Lined Ghettos "Tell Me That Music You Are Most Afraid Of, Now That You Are Here"
Grist "Cody, Can You Recall The Topography Against this Light"
Guernica "We Are So Illegal"
Knockout "As If Two Parts of the Same Hinge"
Lake Affect "Who Has Not Asked, Stay"
Now & Then "Ode to Nobody You Know"
North American Review "Myrrh"
The Offending Adam "Labored"
Pea River Journal "I Am A Forty"
Rock &Sling "No Forwarding," "In the Air, a Door"
San Pedro River Review "Apology Note Left On a Still Warm Pillow"
Sentence "Confessional Poem"
Storm Cellar "All Beautiful Things Mourn You Who Stood Alone"
Sugar House Review "In Another City"
Southern Indiana Review "Against Grief"

Some of the lines quoted in the poem "Elegy from Another City" are from the poem "The City" by the great Greek poet C.P. Cavafy.

"Late Summer Furious Song" owes a debt to the poems of Joseph Millar and James Wright.

SCYTHING GRACE

In the Air, a Door

There in the East Side sky the refinery
coal smoke—a few sentences scribbled

in black ink. A few sentences of dirty sweetness
the day has given.   To grab them from the near-dusk

and take them into the chest. At the bus stop the Sudanese women
are laughing in a language I cannot even name. *I have written this*

so many times, the tongues I cannot translate. Years before I was
an essay. Now there is only the music of the morphine

I find in her mouth. Dark vowels I swallow. The sirens of police
 cars

cast a bloody light. Her ex-boyfriend is in prison for possession.
He was infected. We still receive his old bills.

On the corner is an abandoned house where the junkies
nod their sleepy heads. What is the dance of dying as the spoon
 burns?

She can't wash the scars away. She told me this, a kind of sorrow

soloed: She learned to grasp the light that hums and borrows.
On Parade Street a girl waited on the corner outside the bar.

She was not waiting for a car to slow, to turn a trick.
After a few minutes her boyfriend rode up the block

on his yellow bike, the stem of a plastic rose dangling between his
    teeth.

How can we ignore the ugliness to embrace the unexpected? To
    erase

the black ink of bitterness. *The obituaries we carry.* I have written
        this before.
I have read the texts. I have spoken to the drunk boys in the bars

of nothing. We speak of nothing. We eat the hours to forget
the dead end jobs. Once, in Pittsburgh in a Karaoke bar

I watched a dark skinned woman in overalls open her throat
and unhinge the door in the air

a door she walked through and everyone, everyone followed—

Poem Not Titled Elegy in my Other Windowed Room

I once wrote a poem called *Elegy in my Other Windowed Room* which was an utter failure. I couldn't find the language for what I was feeling long ago in a one room apartment high on valium and weed and my neighbors upstairs arguing again, and the radio playing this strange song by Radiohead that sounds as if whales were singing or a song that whales would write if they had hands to hold instruments, or the song my daughter's doll might hum if she had a voice, though she has a narrator at least as my daughter whispers, *baby takes nap* or *baby sleeping*, or *baby won't sit*, and drags her baby one armed limping like a wounded-bird-doll across the floor—she is learning something here, assigning these feelings to things, much as the writer in me does, when she pulls the baby doll's head right off its shoulders and hairless it rolls across the hard wood floor, rolling like the nine ball I saw my friend Randy send across the felt toward the corner pocket in a big money game, and the head like the nine ball and the nine ball like the head just keeps rolling but then somehow as if an invisible hand touches a finger to it, it stops, the doll's head stops just before it hits the wall, the way that nine ball stopped just short of falling in the far right corner, and Randy stood there dumbfounded, silent before he ran up to it and yelled pointing *you fucking whore, you dirty fucking whore.* And this is the point in the poem it would be beautiful to say the ball fell in, fell in at the moment of his worst despair—that ball not emptying his pocket so much he didn't have gas to drive home, but it didn't drop. Because that's how it goes: things don't fall when they should and break apart when they shouldn't and don't come back together again. Like me and my son's mother a decade ago—how our words failed us, rearranged us, and I lived with him in that room without walls, and the shouting through the ceiling a hard rain to pummel me like the words his mother and I hurled, and how without a car I carried him through the snow to that dreaded day care, the kind of place where only poor people have to send their kids, and the fat white woman there who I knew was not nice, who months later was fired for tying a two-year-old's laces together and laughing as he tried to run, and how a part of me died every time I had to leave my son there. And has been dying ever since. And perhaps you are wondering where this is all going? Going to say, perhaps something about the rain outside falling across the city streets, and the empty tracks, and the train trestle where boys still spray paint the names of their lost lovers, and their dead. My daughter is now talking to her baby doll's decapitated head. Cooing to it as if it will speak.

In Another City

You try to tell me this dream left fingerprints on the cold bottle in your hand, barely standing. Barfly with its other bright edges, sing me a gnarled rag, a piece of paper that says, come home to become a bell. We could be orphaned, we could be like factory smoke in the sky spread over the eastern city, full of grandfather stories and flowering sunflower fields. How less the light pouring through the window at the bus station, the girl syringe thin whose face was a portrait or my own reflection? Someone I knew from long ago. Do not assume there is a light-switch inside a wound that when you flick on reveals the parking lots behind the tracks, and the abandoned warehouses and the stolen mattresses, the floor littered with re-used needles. What wrist is tight there, wanting to undo the tourniquet around your own life but you cannot even find your hands, laying face up in your lap. I want to ask you is there another life inside this life no matter, the tattered one "you fold and unfold and refold like a map." The worn creases nearly torn even when you don't look, it is still there, the path backwards to the empty rooms, as if I was a stranger, all brazen even to myself. I hear things. That there is a book somewhere with copies of your face. Smudged fingertips. Someone is typing your name. Behind locked doors that should have been terminal.

Stenographer of the Damned

The tapping of the keys: failure
of a woman's face on a bus pulling
out leaving you behind; at the counter,
the waitress wipes her hands
on her apron—at this hour
when the bureaucrats
are in bed and the janitors
are wringing out their mops,
the floors of a hundred office
buildings shine in a terminal light.
I can't stop transcribing this terror—

Against Grief

Today I sat in the backyard. The sun on my forehead was cool as a cool hand. When I was a boy. And my mother took my temperature. How in that moment I knew I would not die. The same way I watched a blurry dragonfly hover above my daughter's head. It was a visitation. She reached up, laughing. No one in any of the other backyards. A neighborhood of day shifts. Trains in the distance, the sounds of traffic from the boulevard. The wind was just enough that we needed jackets. You want me to tell you something more? Don't you fucking get it. Yes, I know you do or you wouldn't be here. *Because we've been broken.* Because I was sober. Don't say anything. Receive me as I receive myself. Nothing was shattered. My daughter was running across the long dead grass. The sunlight was absently everywhere.

AN ARRIVAL LIKE AN AXLE

An arrival like an axle. An arrival like a folding chair. Summer lawns and big hats and aunties singing hallelujahs, that kind of arrival, full of fanfare, invisible trumpets in the air, or a summertime kind of long yawning arrival, all lazy and libidinous. Knock-kneed girl kind of arrival, all awkward and full of expectations. Or an old man kind of arrival, cane walked up to your door, just the astonishment of still alive. An arrival is a door to walk through. The one that is waiting is at the train station. An arrival always brings its shadow. Stretched into two. There. And I. And a you. The arrival of your sleeping hands. Departure is a dying ember. Departure never asks why. Arrival is the smell of cut grass. Random patterns like the clouds. I knew not to wake her. I knew someone might read just to keep going. And what if you are the stranger? Then please, I must offer you this chair.

No Forwarding

"Love. Someone from whom to hide."
—Killarney Clary

everywhere I go *I am another*—too

becomes a stranger *is* not a *whether*

but a when there is a door

& a voice that calls I am *a spectator*

of the life I left

you for I am sightseeing such

aloneliness I am traveling towards

my last known address remains your face—

MYRRH

For anyway I meant it, take something, whether a bird's wing or a busted carburetor, or a rusted nail, a shard of broken China. A half dream like ash. Take off my mask. Show me what hollow bone you can make whistle. Invest in me a field of thistles and let your yearning unlearn what thorns have adorned your crown. Unlearn your frown, dusk sobbed for fear. Give me back that gallant year, that talent for sheering the winter's wool. The shapelessness of desire drowns. Haloed, wind blessed, bread smelled, your skin. What you have left is what has been. Been moving through me like a falling shroud through wind. I cannot read the coffee grounds. I cannot hold a cup of sound. I cannot tell the tangled sleep or taxing in the country of my kiss you claimed. For anyway I meant it, take a something least or narrow, large or infinitely sighed, sparrow, egret, grass or grain. This breathing can you feel it? This life, take it, but leave me, some *thing* maimed.

The Literacy of Longing

I have nothing   but your crooked shape

that you've thinned   like an empty honeycomb

widow of evening light   drowsy as a wheat field

you the bread the wine the want for the world   the doors

that must not close   I follow you through

to travel   when we weren't looking

in a waiting room   a window

I turn towards   the unfolding dark

to tell you   everything is opening—

lilacstulipscherryblossoms   the sky

like a palm   and I have come to tremble

                        after years of witness

at the simple way   you tilt your head

as if reading   as if you can almost read

the Braille in the air   between us

LOVERS LIKE STENCILS ON THE WHITE PAGE

Unsung unbearably blue, even frightening

in how they leave us, our responsibilities

among the debris, these utterances

we cannot hold. How even when we go,

anticipating them to *towards us*

with their absence, we are little more

than unassuming formerlies, we are little

more than the weight of falling slow—

SONOGRAM

You want to say the bell to a trumpet. A hollow sound. The sound of
emptiness becoming

whole. Whole as a loaf of bread, and the hungry sound that
echoes.

A sound thin as water? Or deep, deep as the echo of the womb
where the one you thought you would raise was gone,
unexpectedly

on a night of hard rain, when she knelt in the bathroom, the thumb-
sized bloody loss. How many years ago you cannot count except

with your thumbs.

A thumb-sized sound.

That small. That full of losing. How large it grows. And you are lost
in the forest of what did not happen,

searching for the way back to before, but the black birds have
swallowed all of the crumbs.

So you begin again, begin
in the present tense, and the patter of the children
in the fountain downtown, and there is Elmore from the Roosevelt
        hotel
in his wheelchair, the sound of his wheelchair

creaking through the puddles in the moments after rain, and you
    are sitting
there on a bench, not smoking, trying to catch the sound of the
    girls clapping hands
and Elmore raising his arms in the spray of the city fountain, in the
sudden sunlight, somewhere like 6th street, in somewhere where after
the voices stop, you look down, to find the tracks of his wheelchair,
and the sound so long ago that took his legs, the sound you never
heard of his not having legs.

A phantom sound.

Heard our whole lives, for we are all wheeling, with our amputee
limbs, toward that sound of someone so near

you can hear them breathing.

When they are sleeping.

It is not much to ask.

It is not much to ask, *Are you there?*

LABORED

When you left

        the room smelled

like lilies   at a wake

like Patsy Cline

        her later years

that kind   of heartache

that can kill

        is what we *earned*

for the afterlife

        I searched the house

calling   *somehow you knew*

departure

        bloomed

staining

        my body *you*

it is *you*

        I

still

        breathe—

Confessional Poem

I too haven't been born. Because in another version I knew just how you felt. In a small room where friendship becomes almost love like the short one I lost walking home on the road I have not traveled upon. To rewrite what we hate. I want to tell you the night is alone as pushing a grocery cart across the grocery store parking lot at 3 AM. Maybe it sounds better than to keep you apart. Imagine landing on the hard concrete and no one notices? It takes them hours to call the cops. In a hotel you have the room until someone next door leaves out a window. Is there a room inside your chest to confess the disarray you've reached? They wear crosses for Christ and bless themselves on every bank shot. I want to hide inside the untranslated gossip of the Asian-American college students shooting pool. Make it go away. And then the grief begins. We turn it into an into, a wreck to dive, a teaching sigh, for a moment. For everybody is who we are. It is not right we didn't even have enough money to buy candy at the Dollar store or how we found Matt so strung out and sick he shouldn't drink passed out in his own diarrhea, the way I try not to imagine Michael in the hospice, and what we brought we bring we bring nothingless you bring enough for everybody. It is not right we shed our skin. And who was the one who chewed on the edge of the chair, was it Michael who sat in his cage, depressingly unwitty. The drugged haze of late summer. And we had our own entanglement after, the after almost violence need for longing, our bodies becoming tiny Chinese bells, ringing in an opium den. As if looking into crystal ball and saw the sirens. You grabbed the gun. I did not shoot the woodchuck yesterday.

TELL ME WHAT MUSIC YOU ARE MOST AFRAID OF NOW THAT YOU ARE HERE

It is astounding I feel its mouth this morning sweeping, how little the ordinary needs mending, a person notices the body shakes, you can't help noticing its hinges, like butterfly wings, how sometimes what they do is open the sky. And then it came and went. As if to dredge the days, a stream no one noticed until it was a dusty bed. I eat weightlessness and scars, a pity soup I stir and strain and separate the lumps I cannot ascertain. When she was so asleep on the grass—eyes dark as ink that rewrote the page of waking up beside her, her jaw line caught the light as if the world was full of tiny wings, like moths that avoid traps. This life of insects, tiny beings that sing the air with astonishment and annoyance, even fear as when a wasp alights and one must be still. The black and gold thorax gleams the sun. We want to run but hold our body tight as fists. Such appetites insist to leave, the small things die around us every day, against the story we bend like reeds. Tell me— squinting wind-washed white girl wigs and cigarettes, mill town bars and steel toed boots of men who never held your hand, or you in motel rooms and back streets, bone mothered and birds pecking for bread crumbs as if to peck away each word unsaid. In the morning there is the sweeping of the dead. How do you survive abandoned without thread to sew the torn? By what chambered heart so heavy it hurts the skin. As if falling into a nest of wild bees. The body breathing to be born. It loves what opens. It loves what stings.

DRUGS IN PERFECT JARS

The only evidence of that mirage in your pocket
is a crumbled grocery list. In a blue box of probably,
if you are lucky you end up in a part of town
no one recognizes you. Staring at the walls
of the bar so no one imagines how beautiful
it is tearing it down. We are little more than smudges
on a table rasa of paper towels. Perhaps this *is* my
glass downer, my last swallowed pill of light.
Always it's morning in the next apartment,
afternoon in the attic and evening the streets
are full of foreign children, chanting jump rope rhymes—
if we could count the hours of your leaving,
if we could grasp the ache to be included,
that space like a vacuum in the chest,

elusive as water in the hands, an MRI,
a lithograph of the city swept
from your elaborate self, from its crumbling
ramparts of someone else watching the rain
slowly scything through the darkening trees.
How often the almost ones you lost, left
with bitter coffee—dusky orchids,
buried beneath your skin, in your palms
the ghosts of anonymous bodies—trilling away.
in who is yourself a vanishing point
that sang, coming, dignified and dark,
attached in the end to closure. We wake
to water, transfixed to be touched
no one imagines how lovingly—

Who Has Not Asked, Stay

I said it to the grass, to the flame of my open lighter, I said it to the lilies and the leaves. Come to bed and stay. Before the door, a window, at the station, reaching a blessing, stay. Do not go. Such simple phrases in our language. *Stay,* I said to my daughter every year she grew, I lost a part of her. As we lose a part of ourselves. We tremble to stay, we say to the earth river valley meadows the bluffs before the great lake, we say stay do not go like the old ones, the empty husks of steel mills, the empty forges, the ghosts of mill workers walking down Pittsburgh Ave, along the railroad tracks, fossils found along the shore, the small leavings the shells the bass the trout the willow trees. My love with her disease, her swollen hands. *Stay* I ask the Lord even though I do not believe. The sky, the clouds. The road of bikers as they pass me on the highway. The men and women at the corner bar, stay with each other's hands. Do not depart in the morning, for where you go will not be held. Stay we mouth each other's skin like verbs. Stay I say to my thumbnail. When I play an old scratchy Clash album, *when they knock on your door, how you gonna come*, invite them in for tea. Stoned I say stay, stoned too stoned to argue. There is no hurry, I am in no hurry. We can dance till we are missing, till we're tired as housewives, shop keepers closing their iron gates, the boy at the fast food window who had trouble counting out my change, how I wanted to say listen to the lyrics of this song playing, how sentimental they are they could almost save you, like on a Saturday night, moving our bodies to some punk band or disco ball. Without even words, asking each other, *stay.*

The Hour Without Changing is a Long After

Billy Strayhorn drawing a bird on a piece of notation paper
Is said to have prophesized the coming of Charlie Parker *Fool*
Take the damn horn out of your mouth! Miles
Told Coltrane how to stop his solo. *Look, I told myself.*

And closed my eyes.   Even then the sky
Decided it was time to rain.   I like when people whispered,
She's trouble, as if I never saw the scars
On your calves. They are nothing like that.   Figures

In a notebook.   I can't stop hearing noises at night
Since we had the children.   Even the sharks outside
Are scared of our howling wolves.   Listening to Monk
I hear the ache my chest makes

When I watch our daughter run.   She moves close
And whispers, *I have a secret.*   The wind is a secret
Only the leaves know how to tell. Standing in front of Gerhard Richter's
Train tracks I felt small and helpless.   Sometimes when

You open your mouth to me I feel helpless.   Gertrude Stein
Could only be half herself for everyone.   Always the aria
Of our neighbors arguing again.   Sometimes I wonder are we
Little more than cigarette butts flicked out on the sidewalk?

Strayhorn's life as lush as his songs.   Some small dive
We dwell.   Magnificently mischievous, our daughter
Catches us with the hose. *Whoever you are holding me*
Now in hand.   Our grandfather would grin his white beard.

The museum of aloneness, I watch the women come
And go to the Laundromat, folding the clothes
Of themselves. Wearing spandex and bangles. Once Monk
When he was old refused to leave his house before trying

On every hat he owned. It was like that when he played
As if searching for every note ever sounded. Our daughter
Before she first spoke made coos and minor chords
That could have turned into any language. We taught her ours.

Half Past 3 a.m.

What syllable are you seeking Owl, lost or stolen,
in all that furniture you threw
against the wall. The bare bulb sputtered
voices that find you in the distances
of sleep. Speak it. In all these steel gated shops.
The bare bulb muttered in the dark.
You couldn't feel your arms
from a second shift of lifting boxes.
It was 1986 in that tiny room
above the bus station. The moon winks
her glass eye. The moon is a widow.
The moon is probably hungry. The moon knows
Patsy Cline. Her child's poxed face peering
through the window. *She smoothes the hair*
of the grass. She too is alone. The smells
of garbage and cheap cigarettes, your pencils
all sharpened on the desk, your hair all sopping
with her light. She smiles into corners.
Apology cupping his bloody cough. With all the sawdust
on the barroom floor, the shells of peanuts
from the drunks. The jukebox hummed
its quarter songs. No one ever danced.
It was long enough after the war
that people had begun to forget
how terrible it was. When you started
screaming—we couldn't stop you—
the way you did back then, you said your head
                                    was *burning*—.

Daily Architecture Without Hesitation

You are a honeycomb when maybe not,
a dog eared book I was smoking,
or when in the kitchen, a hen, a wren.
Some herbs, or when oregano,
or barely when it was still to vanish
far beyond the pines were we lay
on leaves and autumn light,
when we returned we drank
our coffee burnt, what was
warm was sacred it was our engines
overheating, the sleepless combustion
of our bodies when I was inside you
never sleeping where we'd stayed
awake past scaffolding not speaking
after teeth and tongue. Never full,
the winter evenings drifted
the falling was when your breasts
would rise, your arms an architecture,
your shoulders staircased sigh
I climbed to step inside the hidden
places whether or not I miss you more
than when I was done with missing
you with what we'd made I stir
the only soup I graft the only skin
I gave was what the answer's
missing too the reasons I can't expect
what bridge or ferry we'll forget,
we need bread a hospital a symphony

listening for an entire afternoon.
Did you love well what very soon you left?
This is an older self in short supply.
Give me tender pullings and another,
and I'll give right back
to increase demand, to fight the lack.
This ache of hands I recalled
where you turned your smallness
towards me this mourning
asking for the end of what we were
so many the ones who die
like commas against the sky
I glance up at birds   paused

ELEGY FROM ANOTHER CITY

*The city is peopled
with spirits, not ghosts, O my love:*
—C.P Cavafy

Pale host of daylight moon   the wind balloons

scarves and jackets   tattooed

pierced young   gusting

        into one another's

bodies   basslines

engagement rings   suicide

guitars   pawnshopped

hocked   weather-shorn

spirited   bent backed

old Indonesian man   walking home from the bus

carrying a sack   Cumbia spilling

from an open window   stuffed animals and ribbons

hand written notes   fluttering

from chain-link fences   in place of crosses

where another kid   was shot

And when it came time   to disappear

I raised my hood against the wind   I closed my eyes and stepped

into another country   two blocks

    Whatever I try to do is fated   to turn out wrong   Neon dusked
    bodegas, dead lambs through the fogged glass

    I am footprints of work boots in the snow

I am heavy with grief
                    a certain slant of light

Wherever I turn, wherever I look   Those hours

Of ordinary afternoons

The Puerto Rican barber shop, Jorge sharpening his blade
    The coffeehouse of lost letters

Old women arguing in different dialects buying bread   Italian
    Bakers synagogues

Polish Social Club   The winter sun   These streets
    will never let you go

You will walk them with a cane

The neighborhood of ghosts   The wash board houses, red
    brick factory walls

    for things elsewhere there is no you   Statue of some minor
    martyr

The gypsy storefront with its painted crystal ball   *I see the black*
    ruins of my life, here

Tattoo shop of the dead   Down on the borders of the barrio

Funeral ashes blowing in the wind

I am a seagull swooping for scraps in the shipyard

    day of dull errands   sparrowed mournings   a street at the
    edge of memory

Where is my open tenement door

Where is my gravel path through the shady elms

Where are my tulip trees, my pigeon crusts my bench, Is that my
    voice. *There is a bread that is thick with loaves*

at dusk   dialects muttering in the immigrant grocery

here where I've cathedraled my life

to divine the dark

a single room

shadows of leaves   palimpsest   in the park   on the
pavement

with the homely   hideous disfigured defaced

the only trace   of the light   men once held
        in their fists

through the staff of telephone wire resting at F
        the daylight moon

I Am a Forty

I had a sleep-over with the tide. I wrote your name in shells. I told the low tide I was high. I spied an osprey. I once witnessed a kestrel swoop over road kill and *kreeee*. Sometimes I stop my life to spell AIDS on a coupon to remind myself of Terry or David or my other dead. I knew a nun named Diane who worked hospice until the lost ones changed her. I am a blotter of windowpane, you are my black bread and butter, blue stoop, blowtorch, barefoot peregrine poor rocking on porches in the projects. I am the projects outside in the rain.

Once on East Buffalo Road I stopped and sat cross legged on the curb for no reason. I want shoes without sleep, to run tracks (laps) in your thoughts, the endless freight trains that run through 6th street, as if no day ever ends. How different are jail and communion, like Tory Dent or Tim Duglos who even pencil thin wrote their lives on the walls of the world, eight hour shifts I walked through fields of suicides nameless in a coat made of hungry children. I cannot stand watching animals die, or ponder twelve hour shifts like when the nurses came how many times to change the IV, to die because the doctors failed or didn't care because we are broke.

At night now I play at the pool hall long after closing we keep the lights burning like the cell of a prison or a hospital room. What bars are we kept by? What disease are we trying to cure? What shame? I shoot silently with James, who spent years trying to get clean. Our tangled labor, our lonely mangled acres we can hardly mow.

ALL BEAUTIFUL THINGS MOURN YOU WHO STOOD ALONE

I walk over the stubble of the dead, after the night shift at the factory
of longing and without consolation from anyone I leave.   I hold the
dogwood. I won't forgive the sunflowers. I won't forgive the tulips
who called to you at the train station. I won't forgive the black earth,
or anything that grows. In my hands a knife and a flashlight, I am
searching for your bones in the backyard. I am seeing calligraphy in the
heat lightning that crashes across the sky. I am a footprint and shovel.
I am a yellow cab waiting outside a house with no lights. I want to eat
the dirt with my teeth and spit out glass. I want to eat leather boots
and coal. I want to dig up the back yard till the neighbors call the cops
and come guns drawn asking as I lift the spade to the night to dig for
the moon. The neighborhood graffitis your face. I find it stenciled in
doorways. It follows me on the road. I witness it at every exit.   On
the banks of every lake.   On the trestles and the three bridges.   On
the Susquehanna and the Allegheny, the Ohio, the Detroit River and
carved into our cherry tree: high up in the blossoms veined as arteries,
streetlights, headlines—to the sound of traffic over the back yard, you
are a lullaby. You'll bring light and bees. I am to blossoms like a child
is to fragile. to become other. How sometimes it wasn't drugs. A word
soft as opium breathed in the window of a Laundromat where the lost
clothes are tossed in a bin. To be found never lasts forever. And you
are the chair I sit upon. You are the table and the ink and the child's
broken truck and the gushing fire hydrant water. Or the point right
before. You were. That is enough. This is how I measure loss: I map
the lines across my face. I watch the neighbor children grow. The
curtain pulled across the moon shines so with human loss I left so long
ago. I drink vodka from a paper cup until I burn in the furnaces I can't
stop feeding—

We Are So Illegal

Since friendship darkening from its last stop it's overcast there is music
that reminds me of the wind blowing over plastic café chairs. What
is hidden is not even an echo.
Like a subway's strung out irreverent sentence, the lyric home
inside the tunnel. When you sleep I sometimes catch a few pieces of
your dream as you breath them out. They fall out of your mouth like
puzzle pieces that don't quite fit together. Or are they just missing the
other, like the shape of an open hand reaching to interlock fingers.
My enemies are too young to take me seriously.
How many years our tremulous wail on the same mattress? Wind
washed with thistles. We are so illegal.
Some part of us is a pair of shoes left at platform's end. The birth of
sometimes I forget. The rain in the next room is a lullaby to love, to
loss. To say these words like a slogan, or a billboard outside the hotel
of indifference.
To shine a neon sign in a foreign language outside
the window of your life. I would like to advertise your eyes or to have
them weaved by dark haired children on a 19th century loom, on a
tapestry that with one look will give every worker girl a raise. I would
like to advertise your mouth, the one that could shame any foreman
into lowering his tongue. I would like to point or pout that peace
is close to precipice. One precedes the other and the other precedes
the end. If I
rubbed against the wall of the room we once shared, what would I
apprehend? The archipelago of our limbs navigating across the bed
we sold, the ocean of the torn blue sheets. To sustain just one song
erases misery. When I read you Ahkmatova and you held your face
in your hands. We are a city of broken umbrellas, caught in a squall.

Wind or winde toward rhyming us rough. Your mouth is the mouth you make when you drink from a water fountain. When I read you Tsevateva "your name—impossible—kiss on my eyes." Skinning garments, we've arrived. Let it come. A tenderness both long and loud.

This Ongoing Elegy to Everything

For you are wanted always inside me. The hunger of the black veil. The dirt in my shoes is the same dirt they will toss a handful of me over. When we enter down enough to rise to suck there is no such thing as shape, ourselves. You are anywhere near on all fours. Whatever can ashamed our breathing. Sometime I think my feelings are a gyroscope. When I watch her run I know I could take a life. The saddest looking man came to my door today to sell life insurance. To undo the days of not loving ourselves. Nor a gathering of apples. You are damselfly nor bee. I once passed my friend Zoran's death on a Balkan mountain. There'll be no laughter until the bills are paid. Or the sense of an aftertime. They arrive in the morning when I open my eyes. Flowers on a roadside shrine. Last night we shut all the windows, withholding nothing. Some I know carry 700. I carry seven deaths every day. I've given up counting the number of foreclosures in the neighborhood. Or to begin again with a fact: Isn't every great poem an utter failure? We often go for words like faith, or joy, or despair, how little do I read a little poem about shame. They were the color of saffron rice. On the bus today I couldn't stop staring at the old man's yellow teeth as he talked. You are the blue geometry of a skyscraper against the winter sky. *There is no more lighting of the lamps.* The imprecision of poverty. To forsake the glorious life for the ordinary. Do you remember when our daughter dreamed, her dovelike coos? Come be my acrobat. We are a Big Top of words to write the circus of our days. Do you ever imagine that man walking with a brown grocery bag has a human head inside it? This is what they say to us. To see some who didn't as the one who had. You know Sonny Rollins stopped playing in public for years to translate the birds on the Williamsburg bridge. As if another face only inches begins to unfold itself into description. The abstract feeling as when I watch the starlings. To unstitch the binding for a sort of collage. As if there is another book we endure. The art of notating the awkward and the swooned. Our daughter the folly of day lilies, celebrant of all things short. The smell of Chinese food floating around the corner where a child kicks a ball. Taxi cabs, and subway musicians. In the beginning anywhere in the city you occurred somewhere. Behind door number two? If not for my shadow, today I would not have seen another human figure. Read slowly: there must be something here to save you.

As If Two Parts of the Same Hinge

When we rise, we will fly over the places we loved most, or least.
For you I'd cut my strings like a kite who has found itself tumbling
across your stormy sky. When I take a breath these days I know I keep
breathing for our daughter says a marriage can never fail completely.
Yellow finches chattering on a telephone line. There is no punctuation
mark that can send the signature or her where should when a sentence
steps out of this world and enters the next. For you intensely unhurried
understand this. We made her digging through the dirt. For you there
like a song like wild sage, or an afterlife, like sunflower. For you and
I are not the earth asleep but the dark itself we reach through towards
one another. As if two parts of the same hinge.

ODE TO NOBODY YOU KNOW

Inside the stucco walls of The Mall you work the second shift at the Sports Bar. In the suburbs of the dead. Elbow-deep in the stench from the dish drain, the burning oil from the fry-0-lator. You are altered in so many ways. Your hands are scars from years of hot pot burns. Your hands are something that might raise a hell out of something holy, not that sympathy goes nowhere—chop suey (managers cursing) in the air, what does that take from a man? Year after year, scraping hot wings and sauce on aprons, we in the kitchen spin little umbrellas and stick them behind our ears. We dance burlesque filling orders. Peacocks of the dented pans and trays. After work we drive to the park and drink along the Susquehanna. River of steel and coke, river of your father's night shifts. The portable radio grooves—curses spilling out of the mouths of old men on the stoop. Beneath the Salsa fire-escape of spiraling slang. Why can we only see happiness when it's on fire? The night is never everywhere. And now, far off in the fragrant darkness, the trees are tremulous with bloom.

WITHOUT MEANING TO

The sentence at the end   of the question mark

                               the miniature churches

translating their secrets   dogwood crabapple

paper birch cedar   her mother died nameless

among the trees   she asks why every morning

by the window   the whiteness that comes

through one's face   looking at what

on the otherside   they were

POEM WRITTEN IN THE MARGIN OF AN ECLIPSE

A hallway of maps leading nowhere. He left his brothers Canada, Nick, and Jorge with the drunken cooks in the parking lot of the pool hall. An anthology of bus stations. A flowered urn. At the edge of the city, wondered if after he left they were arrested. After 3 AM. Into a house of runes. For having too many tattoos, too many guns, too many blades, cues, and my life is an unreleased old school record. An unfurnished room, a mattress flopped on the floor. For having too many cartons of cheap reservation cigarettes in their trunks. For being as quiet and unnecessary as is necessary. An anthology of train station goodbyes. For having too many lit telephone wires at the same time. For having too many kids at home asleep in their bed with one parent. For counting out their winnings from the Preakness and their losses from the Pacquio fight. Tonight, eating his tongue—was he arrested— the kind of man who would try to sleep with your wife, and fail, not of resolve, but because he drank too much. Not in the living room or beside the empty clothesline. Maybe they were arrested in the company of crickets, or in the stained glass light found in an *Encyclopedia of Submerged Cities* for the same reason a scene like this rarely exists in American poetry, with its verses about vacations to Mars or Majorca or the lawn at Princeton. For the real poem is always being arrested. Some critic is narcing on this one right now. Even the moon is in handcuffs? In her leather panties. When we paint the moon in leather panties. Let them gawk and ponder. We have no map to offer. To travel our weeping labyrinths.

Canning Sardines (Slavic Grandma Holds the First Sky Over the Next)

Baba hands me the scythe of the strange sentences. Another elegy inside Baba's silver transistor radio of old country. Baba shows me the world as the track curves takes me to the tin tool shed. *Killed without reason* then Baba feeds the birds on the invisible bits of chopped fish. Baba takes a pill: what is Baba a noun or a verb she orchestrates flowers. She sews our secret dead what is it in Baba that feed them, by hand flare stack rising makes Baba brush you tender don't shake who will dig out dirt tight around your Uncles' shoulders, shadows move the knife, Baba packs the oil's distillation the tiny tin. Baba only buries the bodies' excess, their scales and tails. Maybe there are two skies? One to fall through, one to climb? Which one is hidden in the middle of Baba, dusk singed— what fire at the mouth of every forgotten killing field?

Apology Note Left on a Still Warm Pillow

I could not leave the children.
Please forgive me your voice,
for not rushing to the hospital
when your brother was sick.
Please don't blame me that
I've got you correct so seldom,
for pulling only a few threads
away from your veil.
Things could be worse.
I swear by the two blonde
cleaning ladies we witnessed smoking
and laughing over their mops.
Is that your cell phone ringing?
Excuse me did you call?
No one's alarm is set
for mourning. Can I have three
quarters for a cup of coffee?
But that's a mirror a My My My
in the dark, a note to give to runaways
in train stations for sleeping
through the florescent light. Goodbye.
I could have kept you company.
Goodbye like the carved bench names
now long grown into men, women
working the nightshift at the Heinz Factory.
I walk the empty streets for a sorrow
that knows how to tango
beneath the bridge. Forgive me,

for carrying my brown paper bag
of bullshit. I was bringing it
to an old friend I heard
has gone back for rehab,
three felonies toward a cell,
a lifetime ago. What I've learned
is that memory can be faint,
like the glint of starlight. Or a branch
of blackberries by the iron works gate.

UNTRANSLATABLE AUTOBIOGRAPHY OR EMPLOYMENT APPLICATION THAT ENDS IN BIRDS

A torn autobiography. Slips of paper. Your story not his life, but his life. Like that wet bruise of sweeping leaves. An entrance to a once Grand Theatre you cannot find.   Like off Route 20, the statue of Saint Francis feeding sparrows. The sky behind you. Then turn left at the corner where the neighbor boy Ernesto was shot. The street side corner shrine. Crayon scrawled laments on sheaves of notebook. The letterhead for the dead. We drive behind the tricked out Ford Explorer, radiating lights and chrome, bass speakers booming. A pocketful of meds. Where to score is the center of everything we were. Autumn light onto the graveled curve of a bell's vibration, a form of falsetto, the lost voices down the Refinery Road where we found each other's faces. You and I are slow as a tanker marked "biohazard," another form of letter from an alphabet we cannot read follows us. When I am alone there is almost nothing I can spell except in starling. The calligraphy of the sky we write our names with burnt out matches. I sleep in the parking lot while you are far away behind smoked glass drinking Chinese beer at the strip mall. What passes for our lives after we turn into the dirt lot full of junked cars, to meet the man in front of an open shed? His yawn stretches like a hayfield to a barn cooking crystal meth. *Between out and outer now between out and in, between is it between in, and inner?* Mourning is cold like a job you fail to fit in at. What loss lingers as if a bridge across a chasm, the mist is always Gothic. The text a diary, views invisible scarecrow mountains, a back road you might not make it out of. How the man points where he scattered your mother's ashes with the others. Lying in bed I think about your employment applications. Who has help to offer, hands like green prayers. A lesson like bones through skin. What letters for these losses? An empty notebook is like a glass waiting for water, or a wet field waiting for the plow. A psalm is for the throat or for the palms? Three years of orchids left on wet stone. I am still checking my unshaven reflection seven years after my grandfather stopped breathing. When we sleep are chests a rose, the past of rise and fall? Autumn leaves palimpsest their shapes into the ground. It's difficult to bring back these stumps of grief, this odd memorial of every doused candle. A magnolia is the bread we made, I open the pages of petals to the assigned book. A lily to mark the page. Looks like a crack. In the wall of a prison cell. The self that is. Look down: we are something else mixed up. Look out at the stars, the shouldered bay. Maybe this is another of her odd gifts. Here for the honeysuckle, the dogwood blooms: And the fading taillights of her. To see the if, on a damp, gray afternoon. But all I have to hold is what I've lost, I fall down too often. I am often afraid for whoever is unimportant. It is not for nothing we bend to fill out the questionnaire In the official rooms beneath florescent lights. Where the certificates are signed. We doodle clown faces in the margins. Shiny as a noun. The final act is never who you are or how you are but *now*—a red Ford pickup truck swerves in the oncoming lane, scattering finches.

LATE SUMMER FURIOUS SONG

"And gallop terribly against each other's bodies."
　　　　　　　　　　　—JAMES WRIGHT

1

What's engraved on the cypress
　　　above the cold creek, you hang
over a spine of catfish bones?

What is the road you're building
　　　like an ant pushing its crumb
of bread?　What is the barometer

for bullshit, the clock that tells
　　　the deadline for corrupt
cops, greased bearings of dockyard

workers dawdling overtime after dusk
　　　or at daybreak, black blooms
of an El Camino whirring

inside you? Are you hard-wired
　　　to the moon's lament, the praying
mantis lifting its prey, the light

languishes, stacks burning brick,
　　　its pure spun copper cables
stammering out *America.*

2

You were raised humping in a nest of wasps,
        you navigated the Appalachians
with eight cylinders.

On the ground in pans of oil—
        like everything else of combustion,
your carapace of bone

carved by dust and wind.
        There's a burning coal
fading in your throat

from the huge mills by the river,
        you sing to bell housings,
your life is a horror movie

played over and over,
        or a Mexican soap opera
watched by her in the Motel Six.

Along the endless highway
        you hear your voice tooth-geared,
grinding outside an ash tray window sill,

you make a vow to nothing,
        why should you? To work
as you work is not to pray,

endlessly you follow the Monarchs
        through the fields of milkweed.
Digging you find the wild potato,

the root. As though you could tap
        your way from one room of machines
into a forest, river, the wet lands

where we ran, to be free.
        Is there even a shot glass
worth of light to swallow?

3
Our dead preceded the cicadas singing.
        Through the mud of words to another sky
inside this very sentence where a lost sister

wakes in the morning's throat.
        Of the strikebreakers we call scabs.
Fire with no roots, grooved steel

running all night to Binghamton, Wilkes-Barre,
        the ghosts of Gettysburg still muzzle loading,
fire of the profit line we fished, swapped, fire

of diesel, axles, fenders and rubber burned.
        Pawned fast asleep in the arms of near
everything under the ashes and slag, for cash,

for the coke refinery, strip mined, fracking,
        dozers and loaders, she waiting in my truck
while you pissed. Bright tongued

what all you owed and owned was never her,
        including the books you stole,
you thought you owed her,

which all she wrote you, you filed
        in the library of dead letters.
There is a voice that scythes

over the fields and barbed wire fences,
        the voice that holds up
day old foals, curves around an El Camino

engine hoisted on concrete blocks,
        a lament croaked into a whiskey jar,
chain hoists curses, and our nightly furious

kind of love pistoning headlong suicidal
        into the dark of each other's bodies, we call out
our names like white-hot ingots.

ORPHANED

I found a dead yellow jacket. I wished it was a sea. I am blind sometimes, so I wait for the dark. Once I was in a mental hospital waiting by the insane prisoner. We lit our cigarettes in this tiny hole in the wall. If my life is an abandoned farm house at night I stare through the beams of my roof. I stare passed the fabulous constellations. Nothing that is not alone interests me. A goodbye as if said from a great height. I search for you, my orphaned star.

Cody, Can you Recall This Topography Against the Light

beneath the skin, all night Laundromats
& street sweepers brushing away used needles,

we ran when doorways spoke with pipes & pants unzipped
in alleyways, a girl's voice echoes B

or A or D it was only the heart stuttering
guests in the hotel of our own bodies

by the last margin of description where the river
& far off daylight whitens like milk

for another orphan, rending & yielding
must kneel before, as barges loose

glittering mineral freight & cargo holds
gleam with fractures in my voice my face

is naming what is lost, creased & swollen,
because I have not mended. Many days

I cannot make a sentence
while others go for work or barter

underneath the bridge or industrial Flats
where we parked getting high

amid the shrouded languages of illegals
the radio tuned always to the station

blooms for years abbreviating names
to schoolyard monikers replaying games

with chalk lines & counting pigeons
& eleven o'clock news stories

about another gun downed, chrome
spit shinned El Camino, Mustang

roaring down the boulevards of dread,
or nearby jailbreak from County, who

one day from parole just walked away
from the field where they were made to work,

they caught him. Plow-piled as he tried to race
and woke up

dead. Is there anywhere we can run, fly
like V's of geese wide as our mother's arms

of light framed rearranged
to the obligation of the hustle impeded

offering sanctuary? Or something clutched
in both fists, keening

sparrows, I believe that language
conjured to protect us. *Witnessed fragile feathered.*

Another prays daily, in the mirror.
Whole years *folding iridescent wings,* the half alive

calling to any passerby, with voice
of blade & trigger, the night of want

speaks to you through narrow rooms
where bodies tremble with mute desire, beneath a sky

criss-crossed by phone wires
where kids sling the sneakers of their dead.

SCYTHING GRACE (AFTER DYBEK)

We peed in a cup. In the blue barn
we took off our jeans. Was it then
or later when you took off
your belt said, "I have demoted
the last loop of my belt." . . . .
It was late summer and we were racing
on the back roads; mutilated carcasses
of possums and raccoons
littered the barbed fences.
We fed each other yellow petals
as we trespassed the edges of farms,
fucked under full oak trees.
At the edge of the starved fields,
no rain for weeks. We drank
straight whiskey from glass jars
in your father's garage and stole
the ax he kept, we chopped down
mailboxes and dumped them at
the creek. Walt bombed the bass.
We two handed a concrete brick
through the Laundromat glass,
the one where the attendant refused
to give us change. What we did
they blamed on gangs of boys.
The haunting voices never stopped,
the ones that poked through our skin,
the way light perforates aluminum
siding on a trailer. We were expired

license plates hung on the walls of drop outs—
and each week we stood up to pee in the cup.

But sometimes stoned we kept still,
we were still as a possum waiting
for the dread to pass by.
We fooled our parole officers.
A blank piece of paper
nailed to an official looking door. I saw trails
when I drove, squinting my eyes
defiantly at red lights. Suck the lime
and spit out the seeds. Walt
who went like a wind torn sack.
Of what we lacked to hold us down.

You passed me the tab in the public
restroom, the only test you said
you ever passed. We sold
our stash. We bought her clothes
at Wal-Mart, a tiny pair of boots.
We chewed sunflowers seeds.
We looted carnations from gas stations,
twitched ourselves into warm heaps
of laundry, Amaryllis
and beautiful braids of blur,
we woke up folded like origami cranes.
You wore a dress of yellow
mums. Queen Anne's lace in your hair,
rose water sweeping in arcs.
We were lean and hungry

and lost and we picked ourselves up
and where we walked was worse.
We bought her clothes at
Wal-Mart, a tiny pair of boots.

August high summer, Bomb the Bass,
anyway the cursed country terrible
whatever was one cigarette we shared,
walked through cheap apartments
lilacs asking rent, walls like rice paper,
we heard the neighbor's fucking.
Walt wallowed that industrial town
honey with white bread and coffee
and chrysanthemums. Wilting
beside our pancakes (and what auburn
ghosts into a town where I stole and sold
the gay bar Queen's corsage,
in the epic search for who she was, once
again white clematis shaking your tail feathers.
We were steeped in Johnny Walker Red,
buds were dying grace.   We flattened white lilies
between the pages of books,
to coronate the dead we were.

And then you began to bleed—
on the rusty iron loading dock
at a truck stop along Highway I-80,
catalpa buds, the two stoned girls,
one in a red tank top around her half
shown aureole,

who took us home and gave us tea.
We understood the history
of losing things, your breath
bloomed white peonies.
The standing vigils, peeing into a cup.
Toward October she was gone, a smudge
of memory, a bloody stain
written on the mattress—her never-name
calligraphed by our bruised bodies.

TRIPTYCH FROM THE DICTIONARY OF DEAD LETTERS

1

The story goes to what geography? What map? Is there a way except under the river, the tunnel someone else has dug? Fresh plowed dirt. I stopped listening to the city's vast ruins. In my deafness I became an *it,* not a person. A person must ride the bus. A person must hear the orchestra tuning. Moses weeping in some mother cursing out her man in Spanish at the corner store. I walked through the lit streets gambling. What I witnessed made death possible. An I at night, & at that hour, alone, I stopped hearing myself, & everything outside of myself sighed.

2

Once, is to say when before. Of spring wind lifting a newspaper, a fragment of headline. Is that all we are? Or even less? Above the lights. The money you placed there and lost. The streets wet. And shining. No sounds. When I saw my daughters be born. After each I heard the sucked. How often what is loudest never makes a noise. I thought this world must be outlined for someone missing, like a body described in chalk, how final. The street Sweeper clearing away the night's debris. That night, vanishes, slightly injured. To say it as if in parentheses. Can you hear the aside, out of respect I cannot be direct, as the elusive is witness. High as gang graffiti on an overpass. On the bus out of town, a formless face in the window, like a funhouse mirror. A shadow peering around the seat. A girl coloring, copying down her letters. To go on if no one died. As if this isn't the whole story. As if the essay of our life is not also the notes illegible in the margins.

3

The body's grief is brief. A cord of light. Tell me a word like clinical, a thing like vacuum. How *would* you say it laughing. Some new sad conjugation. Someone is missing. Do you get it, not my story. The easy close. To say the word decision. Downstairs tenement, three stops to nowhere. Or how once I tasted plums in the market, I swear she was there. Or in the spring rain. Or in the sparrows eating bread. The rows of grapevines blooming. And where I'd never held her was a shadow, the she is gone. A House a long time after weeping. The susurrus of traffic, voices, the racket, your face afterwards I could not fathom. Even a pronoun. To say the pronoun she is to take the step towards apprehension. She was almost here. In every child after, what shadow sister runs with them? Some days, like Eurydice. Her small shapeless face. What remains is what was ceased. The not knotted cord. The unheard cry, a chord of she, never to be percussed.

Your Voice is a Right Cross

your voice is a right cross, a feint, bodies swaying in an afterhours joint, the last song on the radio of summer, a voice of autumn mountains and sea, the great lakes Erie, the moment a heron rises out of the tall grass, or how your hand becomes a tulip, your body a field of wheat, my mouth threshing slowly across your plain, or quietly smoking on a fire escape, unfolding our bodies like origami cranes, so after there are the lines of where we held. We carry those invisible seams throughout the day. And how in the house of done, the house of leaving, the house of left, something remains. Another kind of music, embroidered in the threaded air, in the sentiment of a lover's look or the sound of freight trains coupling, or the long drive up to Detroit, passed the factories of men making machines, there is that sound, that voice, a sort of hum, in a bar in Cleveland where I sat with tired men, watching a hockey game, cheap beer, I heard it curling under the stools, in the surety of there was nothing much to say, or once in the face of a young woman working the counter at Macey's, when I handed her my bill, a small glance she gave that said nothing more than life is hard and the rest of my day is long a long shift and thank you for being polite and here is your change, it is this inside the concertina the woman plays on the sidewalk, the coins I give, the chords she gave, a system is a room of shadows in whose silence there is something almost a sound breezing through the rain black trees, lilacs and cloves, simmering soup, mesquite grilling in a thousand backyards, a day without work and someone's mother spreading mayonnaise on a slice of white bread, cigarette smoked to the mustard colored end of the filter outside of the Plastics plant, the last inhale and puff. Once I saw it written in asphalt, men leaning on shovels, a Sanskrit difficult to spell, their vocal chords of cedar courage word by word sawdust and scythes and I do not understand but can tell it is a blessing not cruelty or grief, though it rises up from the marrow, a dark noise, a dwelling, a place to well, a hook, a punch, and feint, for what sister countering sorrow, straight to the gut of the body hidden, and the voice shapes the air, like a bell, or whether to believe is to pray in my drawer is the holy card of Our Lady locked prison doors release the names on the rounds are rolled as you duck, throw a hook, and then the unending rain, our nights by the open stove as our children slept on the floor, with not enough money for the heat, and how you sang them to billow with your voice of black roses, blue light and trains, our daughter with her hair like roots. What I mean is to say is we have survived, unexpectedly sighed, crowbarred and jabbed, if our arms are a house, how lucky we are we take turns being the roof:

Sean Thomas Dougherty is the author or editor of thirteen books across genre including the forthcoming *All I Ask for Is Longing: Poems 1994- 2014* (2014 BOA Editions) *Sasha Sings the Laundry on the Line* (2010 BOA Editions) which was a finalist for Binghamton University Milton Kessler's literary prize for the best book by a poet over 40, the prose-poem-novel *The Blue City* (2008 Marick Press/Wayne State University), and *Broken Hallelujahs* (2007 BOA Editions). He is the recipient of two Pennsylvania Council for the Arts Fellowships in Poetry and a Fulbright Lectureship to the Balkans. His work has been read on PBS radio in Pittsburgh, Buffalo, Rochester and Cleveland. Known for his electrifying performances he has performed at hundreds of venues, universities and festivals across North America and Europe including the Lollapalooza Music Festival, the Detroit Art Festival, the South Carolina Literary Festival, the Old Dominion University Literary Festival, Carnegie Mellon University, The University of Maine, Sarah Lawrence College, SUNY Binghamton, the University of California Santa Cruz, the Rochester Symphony Orchestra, the Erie Jazz Festival, the London (UK) Poetry Cafe and the BardFest Series in Budapest Hungary, and across Albania and Macedonia where he was translated and published and appeared on national television, sponsored by the US State Department. He currently lives in Erie, PA, with his family, where he works in a pool hall and writes his poems.

Books from Etruscan Press

Etruscan Press Is Proud of Support Received From

Wilkes University

Youngstown State University

The Raymond John Wean Foundation

The Ohio Arts Council

The Stephen & Jeryl Oristaglio Foundation

The Nathalie & James Andrews Foundation

The National Endowment for the Arts

The Ruth H. Beecher Foundation

The Bates-Manzano Fund

The New Mexico Community Foundation

The Gratia Murphy Endowment

Founded in 2001 with a generous grant from the Oristaglio Foundation, Etruscan Press is a nonprofit cooperative of poets and writers working to produce and promote books that nurture the dialogue among genres, achieve a distinctive voice, and reshape the literary and cultural histories of which we are a part.

etruscan press
www.etruscanpress.org

Etruscan Press books may be ordered from

Consortium Book Sales and Distribution
800.283.3572
www.cbsd.com

Small Press Distribution
800.869.7553
www.spdbooks.org

Etruscan Press is a 501(c)(3) nonprofit organization.
Contributions to Etruscan Press are tax deductible
as allowed under applicable law.
For more information, a prospectus,
or to order one of our titles,
contact us at books@etruscanpress.org.